Speech Of James B. Beck, Of Kentucky: In Support Of The Adverse Report Of The Committee On Finance

James Burnie Beck

In the interest of creating a more extensive selection of rare historical book reprints, we have chosen to reproduce this title even though it may possibly have occasional imperfections such as missing and blurred pages, missing text, poor pictures, markings, dark backgrounds and other reproduction issues beyond our control. Because this work is culturally important, we have made it available as a part of our commitment to protecting, preserving and promoting the world's literature. Thank you for your understanding.

SPEECH

OF

HON. JAMES B. BECK
OF KENTUCKY,

IN SUPPORT OF

THE ADVERSE REPORT OF THE COMMITTEE ON FINANCE
TO THE RESOLUTION STRIKING OUT THE LEGAL-
TENDER QUALITY OF THE UNITED STATES
LEGAL-TENDER NOTES, AND REFUSING TO
RECEIVE THEM FOR CUSTOMS DUES,

DELIVERED IN THE

SENATE OF THE UNITED STATES,

JANUARY 21, 1880.

WASHINGTON.
1880.

SPEECH

OF

HON. JAMES B. BECK.

The Senate having under consideration the joint resolution (S. R. No. 49) in relation to United States Treasury notes—

Mr. BECK said:

Mr. PRESIDENT: It has been my good fortune to agree so often with the views of the Senator from Delaware [Mr. BAYARD] that I cannot help regretting that I am compelled to differ with him on the important question the Senate has to consider. I desire to assure him in advance that whatever I may say in opposition to the resolution, against the passage of which I felt it to be my duty to report, and whatever may be my opinions as to the objects and purposes of those who are clamoring so loudly for its passage, I am sure that he is actuated solely by an earnest desire to promote the public welfare and to return at the earliest possible moment to the safe constitutional methods of the fathers of the Republic. I feel, however, that the resolution is unnecessary, unwise, ill-timed, and calculated to disturb the prosperity which, I hope, is dawning upon the country. His proposition is not a new one. It was voted down with unusual unanimity by both Houses of Congress less than twenty months ago. In May, 1878, the House of Representatives, by a vote of 173 to 35, and the Senate, by a vote of 41 to 18, passed the following bill, which was approved by the President May 29, 1878. See United States Statutes, volume 20, page 87:

An act to forbid the further retirement of United States legal-tender notes.

Be it enacted by the Senate and House of Representatives of the United States of America in Congress assembled, That from and after the passage of this act it shall not be lawful for the Secretary of the Treasury, or other officer under him, to cancel or retire any more of the United States legal-tender notes. And when any of said notes may be redeemed or be received into the Treasury under any law, from any source whatever, and shall belong to the United States, they shall not be retired, canceled, or destroyed, but they shall be reissued and paid out again and kept in circulation: *Provided,* That nothing herein shall prohibit the cancellation and destruction of mutilated notes and the issue of others of like denominations in their stead, as now provided by law. All acts and parts of acts in conflict herewith are hereby repealed. Approved May 31, 1878.

That law is a very distinct expression of the will of Congress, and a very clear assertion of its power, in time of peace, to reissue and keep in circulation all the then outstanding legal-tender notes. The President and his advisers had no doubt as to the right and power of Congress to do so. The approval of the act was prompt, and there was no pronounced clamor against our constitutional authority to pass it from any quarter. When that bill was before the Senate the Senator from Delaware moved the following amendment to it:

Provided, That the said notes when so reissued shall be receivable for all dues to the United States excepting duties on imports, and not to be otherwise a legal tender, and any reprint of the said notes shall bear this superscription.

He sustained it in one of the ablest and best considered speeches he ever made; yet only eighteen Senators supported it, and forty-one voted against it. Among the latter were six out of the nine members of the present Committee on Finance, I being one of them. That amendment, it will be observed, is in substance and almost in words the resolution the Senate is now asked to pass. Let me read it:

Resolved, &c., That from and after the passage of this resolution all United States notes shall be receivable for all dues to the United States excepting duties on imports, and shall not be otherwise a legal tender; and any of said notes hereafter reissued shall bear this superscription.

Neither the President, nor the Secretary of the Treasury, nor the distinguished list of petitioners whose gilt-edged and morocco-bound petition is paraded before us with such a flourish of trumpets, nor the bankers, brokers, and bondholders who are so much alarmed lest the country be dishonored and the Constitution shattered by the reissue of legal-tender notes in time of peace, exhibited any of the anxiety they now profess to feel, although these notes were then at a discount, were not redeemable in coin, and were subject therefore to denunciation as irredeemable currency, a forced loan, dishonest money, rag-babies, and the various other epithets which the adherents of the money power in their pretended zeal for the dear people delight to indulge in. It seems to me then was the time, when a new assurance was being given to the people that their money should be maintained at its then volume and that the denomination of the notes should not be changed, for the distinguished petitioners to have given to Congress the advice they now so freely volunteer, and to have pointed out the dangers to constitutional liberty and law and to the best interests of the people for which they at this time so feelingly plead.

Now gold and silver coin of the standard value prescribed prior to July 14, 1870, and nominated as the measure of payment *at the dictation of the money power* in all the bonds since issued, can be demanded and obtained from the Government for the face value of every one of the notes of the United States. The Secretary of the Treasury tells us in his last report that he has over $225,000,000 of gold and silver coin and bullion in the Treasury, nearly $160,000,000 of which is available for all purposes. Other official reports show that the enormous taxation we have endured since the war has produced revenues that have enabled us to reduce the public debt from $2,773,236,173, as it stood July 1, 1866, to $2,011,798,504, as it stood January 1, 1880, being a reduction of $761,437,669. The Secretary in his report December 3, 1877, showed that the maximum amount which it was possible to claim July 1, 1877, as necessary to comply with all the obligations of the sinking-fund law was $475,318,888, and we have been applying all our surplus revenues to that fund ever since, so that it is safe to say that we have exceeded up to this time all the obligations of the sinking fund by at least $250,000,000. These debt statements exclude all the great floating war debt on which hundreds of millions have been paid out of the proceeds of the sales of our ships, horses, mules, wagons, and all the other vast materials purchased out of the appropriations so lavishly furnished during the years of strife. The War, Navy, and Treasury Departments claimed all these things as their property, on the ground that they were charged with them, when the original appropriations were made, and therefore they had the right to use the proceeds as they pleased to pay the debts these Departments owed, and they paid lavishly to their pets and friends in ways that Congress knew nothing of.

Mr. President, if one-half of the vast sums which reached the Treasury in gold (forgetting all that was stolen and squandered) from the taxes taken from the pockets of the people had been retained, instead of being used to pay the principal of the public debt, with the premiums, double interests, and costs of that operation, and the greenbacks had not been repudiated at the custom-houses, resumption would have come of itself years before it was forced on the country. Nobody was demanding payment of the principal of our debt; its burden was diminishing by being let alone in proportion as our wealth and population increased.

The Secretary shows that he has a large and increasing surplus fund from excess of receipts over expenditures, so that all danger of the non-payment or depreciation of the United States notes is at an end. The coin in the Treasury held as reserve cost the people in commissions, expenses, and double interest at least 6 per cent., or $13,500,000. It is worth 4 per cent. per annum, so that it is held at an annual cost of over $8,000,000 in order to remove all possible doubt, uncertainty, or apprehension as to the absolute equality in value and convertibility of these notes into coin. In addition to all this, the Secretary claims that under the resumption act of 1875 he has the power now to sell as many 5 per cent. bonds of the United States from time to time, and at any time he pleases as will enable him to obtain and retain coin in the Treasury to pay every outstanding note on demand. If $500,000,000 is in his opinion (and he is the sole judge) necessary he can sell them; indeed, there is no limit to the security except the tax-paying capacity of the people of the United States. With these vast sums and enormous powers held and given to protect these notes it is absolute folly for any set of men to pretend that there is any sort of doubt that they are and always will be as good as coin. The Secretary, after telling Congress that he can easily maintain resumption with the present volume of notes outstanding, gives the highest evidence of the confidence of the people in them when he says:

The great body of coin indebtedness has been paid in United States notes at the request of the holder. * * * But little coin has been demanded on the coin liabilities of the Government during the same period, (from January 1 to November 1, 1879,) though the amount accruing exceeded $600,000,000.

Yet the New York petitioners, in their gilded memorial to Congress urging that these notes be degraded by having their legal-tender quality destroyed, and that they be forever repudiated by the Government refusing to receive them for taxes at its custom-houses, say:

We believe that this measure, if enacted into law, will encourage every legitimate business enterprise; will revive confidence in permanent investments; will give extended employment to labor in all industrial pursuits; will secure to honest toil its just rewards; will be a sheet-anchor to stability in every department of business, and discourage that spirit of uncertainty which breeds disastrous fluctuations in prices.

The petition is signed by a highly respectable body of men. Governor Robinson, Mr. Belmont, Messrs. Drexel, Morgan, & Co., Mr. Oppenheimer—Jew and Gentile—all the money-kings are there. "*All honorable men.*"

It presents a sharp contrast to the simple petition from the workingmen of Philadelphia, presented yesterday by the Senator from Alabama, [Mr. MORGAN,] which bears the mark of the anvil and the workshops, but is all the more entitled to consideration as an honest protest made against the passage of the resolution, because made by the *sons of toil*, about whose welfare the money-kings appear so anxious. I am glad it is here, so the representatives of the people can consider their case as well as that presented by the distinguished gentleman from New York. I deny all the assumptions of the New York petitioners. I deny that the passage of the resolution will have any one of the effects claimed. Surely confidence in permanent investments needs no revival when our 4 per cent. bonds were at a premium of 3 per cent. the day after the interest was paid, and are over 4 per cent. to-day. Honest toil asks no other reward than a chance to earn the notes as they are; the complaints against and abuse of them have never come from men engaged in honest toil. If any dissatisfaction has been expressed anywhere since the law of May, 1878, was passed; if any petitions to Congress have been presented seeking to destroy any quality now possessed by the legal-tender notes prior to the change of front by the President and his Secretary when this session of Congress opened, or prior to the introduction of this resolution, I failed to observe the fact.

It is always a safe and generally a wise policy to let well enough alone. It seems to me to be both safe and wise not to disturb the currency used by the people when their business, after years of disaster, is improving, and not to alarm men who are just beginning to rally from stunning blows. Nothing proves that to be our present condition more satisfactorily and conclusively than the contrast between the business failures now and for the last few years. I take the following statement from the last annual circular issued by the mercantile agency of Dun, Barlow & Co., of New York:

Year.	Number of failures.	Amount of liabilities.
1874	5,830	$155,239,000
1875	7,740	201,060,353
1876	9,092	191,117,786
1877	8,872	190,669,936
1878	10,478	234,383,132
	42,012	972,470,207

During these terrible years when forced resumption was being consummated over forty thousand business men, *or firms composed of many men*, were swept away, their liabilities amounting to almost half the amount of the public debt of the United States, and forty million of people deprived of one-third or one-half of the value of their property, suffered to an extent that no mercantile agency can estimate, in order to make a few bankers and bondholders rich out of their wretchedness. The same authority makes the following exhibit for the first nine months of 1879, and contrasts it with that of the first nine months of 1878, as follows:

Year.	Number of failures.	Amount of liabilities.
1878	8,678	$197,211,129
1879	5,320	81,054,940

And from the 1st of July to the 1st of October:

Year.	Number of failures.	Amount of liabilities.
1878	2,853	$66,378,363
1879	1,262	15,275,550

The publishers add:

The foregoing figures indicate that for the third quarter of 1879, the failures in the United States have been less *than one-half* than for the third quarter of 1878, the precise decrease being 1,591. The liabilities show even a much larger proportionate reduction, being *less than one-quarter* of what they were in the same period of last year—the figures showing the liabilities for 1879 to be fifteen millions as against sixty-six millions for the third quarter of 1878. It will, of course, be remembered that for the first two months of the third quarter of 1878 the failures were unusually numerous, owing to the prospective repeal of the bankrupt law in September of that year; but, even taking that circumstance into consideration, the decrease in the last quarter is almost phenomenal, in view of the fact that the average number of failures for the third quarter of the preceding four years was 2,003, or nearly double the number of the last quarter's failures, while the average liabilities for the third quarter of the four years was fifty-two millions, exceeding by three times the amount of liabilities of the third quarter of 1879. The figures for the quarter just ended, therefore, add another to the many indications of the wonderfully improved condition of trade throughout the country. For the nine months of the two years the comparison is almost as favorable as for the quarter just closed—the failures for the first three quarters in 1879 being 5,320 in number, as against 8,678 for the nine months of 1878. The liabilities are eighty-one millions for the first nine months of 1879, as against one hundred and ninety-seven millions for the same period of 1878—a reduction in liabilities of more than one-half.

After the people have been compelled by Congress to suffer and endure all these things, and after they have supplied and placed in the Treasury such enormous sums of gold and silver coin to assure all men everywhere that the notes of the United States shall be and forever remain equal to and be convertible into coin, it would seem to me that the crushing of the contraction wheel might cease, and they might at least be allowed a little while without further congressional interference to ascertain whether the prosperity they have so long hoped and prayed for is to continue, or whether with the carrying trade of the country in the hands of foreigners, with protective tariffs cutting off nearly all exports of manufactures and doubling home prices, with enormous debts, Federal, State, municipal, corporate, and individual, upon us, we can rely on agricultural exports alone and continue to prosper. I think the chances are all against us unless we change many of our laws. Much apprehension is expressed by the combinations of the money power, lest the people may rush into wild speculations and again bring about the ruin from which they are just escaping. if they are allowed to use their present resources in the way they think most conducive to their own interests; the wise men of the East seek to constitute themselves the special guardians of the ignorant masses and protect them from all such danger by taking control of the finances of the Government and arranging them so as to guard against overtrading, unwise speculation, and the dangers of a redundant currency.

Mr. President, we have had too much *meddling;* that is at the bottom of all our troubles. If this is to continue to be a Government of the people, for the people, by the people, they must be allowed freedom from the dictation of any class of men, to manage their own affairs in their own way and have a chance to obtain the money which they think is necessary to transact their business. It is the merest pretense that we have a redundancy of currency for the wants of the people, and it is the most arrogant presumption to assert that the regulation of the amount required is safer in the hands of national bankers or Treasury officials than in the hands of the Representatives of the States and people in Congress assembled. Let us look at the first proposition. The monthly-debt statement for January 1, 1880, shows that we cannot have, even if every dollar ever issued was in existence and available for business purposes, more than $750,000,000 in legal-tenders, national-bank notes, and silver of all denominations. The gold is a mere Treasury reserve to secure and make good the other circulation. But call that $150,000,000 more, which is not true in any proper sense. With our present population of fifty millions that is $18 to each individual; without the gold it is $15. How does this compare with the money in use among the leading commercial nations of the world? Turn to Executive Document No. 5, first session of the present Congress, and examine a report to Congress on the state of labor in Europe, made by the present Secretary of State, dated May 17, 1879, and Senators will find that France has eight thousand millions of francs, or $1,600,000,000, in circulation now in gold and silver coin, of which it is not possible that less than $600,000,000 is in silver, and she has over $450,000,000 in notes of the Bank of France, all of which are a full legal tender for all debts, public and private, and each is at par with the other, making a total of $2,050,000,000 of circulation—$40,000,000 more than our whole national debt; and this in a country much smaller than the State of Texas, with thirty-six millions of population, at least fourteen millions less than ours, with a limited seacoast and only 12,720 miles of railroad, while we have nearly ninety thousand miles and an almost boundless continent, containing more territory than all Europe, including Great Britain and Ireland, exclusive of Russia, by 1,240,088 square miles. The people of France have nearly $60 *per capita*, almost four times the amount we have. She is admitted to be prosperous, although she paid within the last ten years $1,000,000,000 in gold to Germany, and was conquered and overrun by hostile armies.

Secretary Evarts shows in that report that the bank-note circulation of Belgium is 661 francs, or over $132, to each inhabitant of that kingdom. These notes are a full legal tender for all debts, public and private. The people of Belgium are among the most enterprising and intelligent in Europe. Their products are found in every quarter of the globe. A few days ago the English papers, corroborating the Secretary, announced that magnificent iron depots and bridges made in Belgium were being erected over the Clyde and in the city of Glasgow. They have a circulation *per capita* of nearly $8 to our $1 and are prosperous.

Mr. Evarts shows further that Germany with her forty-two million of population has a circulation in coin and notes of $714,000,000, or $17 *per capita*, even after she had in an evil hour demonetized her silver, which, prior to the payment of the French indemnity, was her only coin circulation. Her notes are a full legal tender for all debts public and private. She has few sea-ports, only 18,229 miles of railroad, yet her recent distress has been such from the contraction of her currency that Hon. WILLIAM D. KELLEY, of Pennsylvania, in his recently published letters, tells us that the leading bankers in Germany and Prince Bismarck assured him that the country had lost one hundred million of marks, or $25,000,000, by the process of demonetizing her silver, while the general injury to the people and their business has been beyond calculation. He was assured that the sales of silver had been stopped and its use would soon be restored.

I have his letters before me, carefully revised. On page 30 of his letter from Germany he says that he told Prince Bismarck in substance that in his opinion the demonetization of silver in Germany had worked badly, and the reply was:

Yes, in that matter we have gone too fast and too far. We have not been wise. * * * It is clear we did not need to abolish silver money—we should have supplemented it with gold coinage. The sale of silver has reduced the price of that metal, has cost the empire an immense sum, and cannot be continued without ruinous loss, as Von Dechend, president of the Reichs Bank, has shown, and I have therefore prohibited further sales.

After a somewhat detailed conversation as to the probability of a convention of the nations, and as the course the United States would otherwise take on her own responsibility, Bismarck said:

In this matter you must not act alone. Others must co-operate with you. I have told you that no more silver will be sold, and you may also know that the people want the coins for business, and that they will go into circulation again. It is already ordered.

It seems, therefore, that Germany is likely to seek relief from her contraction of the currency, which, though now greater than ours, has by a process similar to that we have pursued brought her people to the verge of bankruptcy. The Secretary shows that the people of Great Britain, numbering thirty-two million in a country less than half the size of the single State of Texas, with only 17,263 miles of railroad, have a circulation of $905,688,000, or about $30 *per capita*, nearly double the amount even now allowed to the people of the United States, yet in the face of all these and many other like facts the moneyed organizations of the East and such newspapers as they control denounce all of us who are unwilling to still further curtail and cripple the small amount of currency we have as inflationists, secret repudiators, and everything that is vile. But, Mr. President, we have not anything like the amount of circulation we are charged with having on the books of the Treasury. For example, turn to the last monthly statement of the public debt made by the Secretary of the Treasury on the first day of this month and year and you will find in making up the sum of $393,711,679 of United States notes, certificates, &c., that we are charged with having $15,674,303.78 of fractional currency in circulation, when in fact there is not exceeding $1,000,000 of that amount in existence. Senators will recollect the debate in May last, when provision had to be made for the payment of the arrears of pension. The Secretary of the Treasury then insisted on having authority given him to increase the interest-bearing debt by authorizing the sale of $18,000,000 of 4 per cent. bonds. The leading members of the Committee on Finance of the Senate sustained him; I and others opposed. We convinced a majority of the Senate that the fund, then about $8,500,000, held for the redemption of outstanding fractional currency might as well be used to pay arrears of pensions as not, and we so applied it. The now known facts have justified our action. The fractional currency presented during the last year has been less than the interest at 4 per cent. on the sum held for its redemption, and it is apparent now that about $14,000,000, perhaps more, of fractional currency charged as outstanding, being one-third of the whole issue, is gone and never can be presented for redemption.

What is now known to be true as to the fractional currency is equally well known to be the fact in regard to the legal-tender notes, though not to the same extent in proportion to the amount issued. The issue of the legal-tenders reached the highest point in 1864 and 1865, when there were $433,160,569 of them in circulation. At that time there was only $22,894,877 of fractional currency issued. That currency did not reach its maximum of issue till July, 1874, when it was $45,881,295. As it is now known that from 30 to 33 per cent. of the fractional currency has perished, it is fair to assume that at least 10 per cent. of the legal-tender notes are gone. Years of war, during which they were paid to soldiers and sailors in dangerous service, followed their issue. Fire and flood have destroyed millions of them. Since the war they have gone through reconstruction and strife in the hands of men unused to the care of money. It is clear to my mind that there is not $300,000,000 of them in existence now. I do not know what proportion of that $300,000,000 is in the hands of the people. In May last I wrote to the Comptroller of the Currency for official information on that subject, and received the following letter, which I then read for the information of the Senate:

TREASURY DEPARTMENT,
OFFICE OF COMPTROLLER OF THE CURRENCY,
Washington, May 6, 1879.

SIR: In response to your request, I send you herewith statement of the Treasurer showing the amount of legal-tender notes outstanding by denominations on April 30, 1878. I also inclose statement of the Treasurer of May 1, 1879, and an abstract of the reports of the national banks for January 1, 1879, the date of the last compilation of their reports. From the statement of the Treasurer it will be seen that he reports the amount of United States notes in the Treasury on May 1, $70,444,823. The amount of legal-tender notes held by the banks on January 1, exclusive of United States certificates of deposit, was $70,561,233. Tables are given in my report for 1878—pages 103, 104, and 106—which show that the amount of Treasury notes and bank notes held by the State banks, trust companies, and savings-banks was, at the dates given, $48,398,738; the amount held by private bankers is estimated at $28,000,000; which makes an aggregate of $76,398,738. If one-half of this amount was in legal-tender notes, then the whole amount of such notes held by banks and bankers other than national banks was, say, $38,000,000; which would give the aggregate amount of legal-tender notes held in the Treasury and by all the banks and bankers of the country, $179,006,000; leaving an aggregate of $167,675,000 held by other parties.

Very respectfully,
JNO. JAY KNOX,
Comptroller.

To Hon. JAMES B. BECK,
United States Senate.

Of course these amounts vary from time to time. I think it likely the sums held now are smaller than those held at that time. It will be seen from the above, however, that there were at that date, some eight months ago, upon the assumption that there were then outstanding legal-tender notes to the amount of $346,681,000, only $167,675,000 in actual circulation among the people. If I am right in assuming that the actual amount in existence does not exceed $300,000,000, then there was only $120,994,000, being very many millions less than there is gold and silver coin lying idle and unproductive in the Treasury, held there under the pretense of possible necessity to redeem them. The statement referred to by the Comptroller as to the denominations of the legal-tender notes outstanding was also read by me, and will be found in the RECORD of the proceedings of May 6, 1879, page 1276. It shows that there were then $100,855,980 of these notes in denominations of $100 and upward, which made them in no sense currency for common use in the ordinary transactions of life among plain people. Of these the Comptroller says $31,940,980 were one-hundred-dollar bills; $31,279,500 were five-hundred-dollar bills; $33,620,500 were one-thousand-dollar bills; $2,005,000 were five-thousand-dollar bills; $2,010,000 were ten-thousand-dollar bills; total, $100,855,980—all of which might as well be bonds of the United States locked up in bank or Treasury vaults as pretended circulation; and these denominations cannot be changed. I have no means of knowing what denominations constituted the $179,000,000 held by the Treasury and the banks. If they were of the smaller denominations they about exhausted them; if of the larger, it still left the miserable remnant I have shown to meet the wants of fifty millions of the most enterprising, energetic, and restless people on earth; yet we are called inflationists if we dare to protest against the further destruction of their usefulness and paying capacity.

In protesting, as I do, against striking out the legal-tender quality of the greenbacks, their further degradation, and the destruction of their usefulness by a new declaration that they shall not be receivable by the Government for custom-house taxes, their receipt for these dues now being, as I think, the wisest and best of the acts, legal or illegal, of the present Secretary of the Treasury, I must not be understood as indorsing or as asserting the constitutionality of the original acts under which they were issued. I have never believed that Congress, either in time of war or peace, had any power to do more than coin gold and silver and regulate the value thereof; and I have always thought it ought to provide for the coinage of either metal upon equal terms and in such quantities as the people may present bullion at the mints for coinage. That opinion I have often expressed in the Senate and elsewhere as forcibly as I could; but the Supreme Court of the United States—I care not how or for what purpose its change of front was effected—decided against my views, and I submit to the decision and make the most of it. I have, since my career in Congress began, seen many laws passed which seemed to me to be in palpable violation of the Constitution of the United States. Reconstruction acts, constitutional amendments, and all sorts of legislation have become parts of our system against my protest; but I sustain them as faithfully now as if I had originally approved them. I have always believed and now maintain that the act of March, 1869, requiring the principal of all our bonds to be paid in coin and repudiating our legal-tender notes was not only declaratory legislation beyond the scope of legislative authority, but a fraud of the deepest dye upon all the tax-payers of the country; yet when the act of July 14, 1870, was passed, authorizing the refunding of $1,500,000,000 of our bonds at low rates of interest, making principal and interest payable in coin of the then standard value, and when they have been so refunded. I admit that the credit of the Government can only be maintained by a strict compliance with the obligations entered into. Disclaiming all intention to be offensive, I may say that I have never believed that the present President of the United States was legally elected to the high position he holds, but no Senator would deprecate more than I would any suggestions looking to the raising of even a doubt now as to the legality of his title. So with the legal-tender notes. They were issued at a time when Congress assumed that the exigencies of the public service required the issue of such notes, and whatever else the Supreme Court has done or left undone, it has never been silly enough to declare either that Congress had certain powers over the currency of the country in time of war which it does not possess in time of peace, or that the court sits as a revisory body over Congress, to determine when exigencies do or do not exist on which Congress may or shall not act. It admits that wherever and whenever Congress can act when an exigency arises, Congress is the sole judge of the exigency requiring its action, whether it be in time of peace or war. It must not be forgotten that in all the acts authorizing the issue of legal-tender notes the following was part of the provisions concerning them:

And any of said notes when returned to the Treasury may be reissued from time to time, as the exigencies of the public service may require.

Congress must be the judge of the existence of any exigency requiring legislation. It may have information even now which the Supreme Court has no right to know anything about as to the objections foreign nations may have to our proposed action in regard to an interoceanic canal, or as to the peculiar relations of the western provinces of Mexico to our great railroad and mining interests. Can the court say we must tell them and publish to the world all our reasons for regarding an exigency as existing, or likely to arise, before we can pass upon questions of currency which in certain contingencies the court would say it was our unquestioned right to do? I deny that the court ever claimed or ever will claim any such power. In regard to the legal-tender notes Congress has, since the war, exercised its discretionary power over them in every variety of form; it has contracted their volume, and stopped contraction; it has increased the amount in circulation, and prohibited its Treasury officials from changing the denominations existing; the act of May, 1878, was perhaps a less notable exercise of the recognized power of Congress than the action taken in 1874. Under the auspices of Secretary McCulloch legal-tender notes had been by action of Congress *retired and canceled* till Congress intervened in February, 1868, and stopped further contraction, leaving $356,000,000 of them then outstanding. In October, 1872, the Acting Secretary of the Treasury issued $5,000,000 in excess of the $356,000,000. The legality of the act was at once controverted, and Secretary Sherman, as chairman of the Committee on Finance of the Senate, made a report, January 14, 1873, proving, to my mind conclusively, that the action of the Secretary was wholly without warrant of law. Some very good lawyers, however, differed with him, the distinguished Senator from Vermont [Mr. EDMUNDS] being one, holding that the act of the Secretary was not illegal.

Mr. EDMUNDS. The Senator will allow me to say that while I did differ with the report on that point of law, I did think the thing itself never ought to have been done.

Mr. BECK. That is true. I merely mentioned it because I saw that in the debate the Senator took part.

Mr. EDMUNDS. The Senator is quite right in regard to the position I took.

Mr. BAYARD. The committee reported against the legality of the Secretary's act.

Mr. BECK. That is just what I want to show. The committee, as the Senator from Delaware says, reported against the legality of the reissue of the five million. That was in 1873, on the 14th of January. But in September, 1873, when the failure of Jay Cooke & Co. alarmed the country and shook public confidence in all bankers, the President and his Secretary of the Treasury, in defiance of the Sherman report, and, as I think, in plain violation and defiance of law, issued $26,000,000 of legal-tender notes in excess of the $356,000,000, on the urgent demand and perhaps irresistible pressure upon them by the money power of the city of New York, doubtless of many of the men who are now so abusive of those of us who do not obey their orders and vote to destroy the notes they caused the then Secretary to reissue to suit their private interests. To avoid such complication, the committees of both Houses of Congress took up the subject when we met in December, 1873. Nearly all agreed that the power claimed by the executive officers to inflate or contract the currency to the extent of $44,000,000 to suit either personal or political interests could not be tolerated. We agreed that this was a Government of laws, and not of men; that stability in the volume of the currency was indispensable to the business interests of the people. The chairman of the Committee of Ways and Means [Mr. DAWES] proposed $356,000,000 as the limit to be fixed; Mr. Ellis H. Roberts, of New York, another member of the committee, proposed $382,000,000, the then outstanding volume, and I, then a member of that committee, proposed $400,000,000 as recognizing the limit fixed by previous laws, and by the claim of right asserted by the President and his Secretary. My proposition prevailed in the House of Representatives by a large majority, as the record will show. Nobody doubted the constitutionality of the bill or the right of Congress to remove the uncertainty which executive action had attached to the volume of currency; expediency alone controlled the votes of members. For example, Mr. DAWES and all who agreed with him voted for the $382,000,000, as proposed by Mr. Roberts. It was clearly as unconstitutional in time of peace to increase the legal-tender notes $26,000,000 as it was $44,000,000. The Finance Committee of the Senate through its chairman (Senator now Secretary Sherman) reported a bill, March 23, 1874, fixing the legal-tender notes at $382,000,000. Although that committee had by its report in January, 1873, demonstrated that $356,000,000 was then the legal limitation, after long debate the Senate increased the committee's proposition up to $400,000,000 and instructed the committee to report a bill to that effect. Mr. Sherman on the 3d day of April, 1874, reported it back at $400,000,000, and it passed both Houses of Congress at $400,000,000. It was, however, coupled with provisions as to banking which the President thought might inflate the currency largely, and he vetoed it, no objection or suggestion being made by him as to the constitutional power of Congress to increase the currency from $356,000,000 to $400,000,000.

Mr. BAYARD. Will the Senator allow me to ask him to complete the history of that act and state that the position which I hold to-day is the one that I insisted on then; the same arguments that are preferred on that side of the question were urged by me in committee and out of committee, in the Senate and everywhere.

Mr. BECK. I desire to say, as I said in the beginning, that I have no doubt the Senator from Delaware in all his acts is influenced by the highest motives of patriotism.

Mr. BAYARD. I did not speak of the motive. I spoke of the fact.

Mr. BECK. I say now that the Senator from Delaware, in my judgment, has been consistent from the beginning to the end in the position he now maintains. In all the votes that he has given, so far as I know, he has maintained the position he is now maintaining; but the Senator from Delaware is not the American Senate, nor the House of Representatives, nor the sole representative of this people, although he is a highly respectable and very able Senator from Delaware. He was overruled. I am speaking of what Congress did.

Mr. BAYARD. All I asked was that the record be stated fully.

Mr. BECK. That is right, and I will not in the course of my speech allude to anything that will indicate that the Senator from Delaware has been inconsistent in any act of his. Soon after the occurrences to which I have just alluded a bill was passed and approved by the President, which was voted for by the present Secretary of the Treasury, fixing the legal-tender circulation at $382,000,000, at which it remained till modified by the free-banking law—that is, free to all bondholders and a close corporation against all others—further contraction under which was stopped by the act of May, 1878. During all these changes the men of the East raised no clamor, saw no danger to the Constitution; indeed, they caused the President and the Secretary to do the only illegal act done. But I need not amplify these well-known facts, nor further expose how hollow the present clamor is.

All the vast revenues collected since the war closed, except customs dues, have been payable, and were generally paid, in legal-tenders, which have been paid out over and over again for all the debts contracted by the Government, (except to the bondholders,) and to all its agents, employés, and pensioners. In this way in the last fifteen years they have, in time of peace, been reissued many times over.

Will any Senator assert that the exigencies requiring the currency Congress authorized during the war, and which the Supreme Court sustained, are ended, or have passed away? Is not the roll of pensioners as large as ever? Did we ever pay in any year as large a sum by $15,000,000 for that purpose as in the year just closed? Have the internal taxes, which were unknown before the war, and imposed to pay interest on the debt contracted to carry it on, been removed? The $116,000,000 collected annually, and the swarm of officials maintained to coerce their collection, furnish an emphatic answer in the negative. Has our once prosperous commerce and carrying trade on the high seas, which before the war brought our people large revenues and profits from other nations, been restored? Our deserted shipyards and the $100,000,000 we now pay annually to foreigners, our commercial and political rivals, to enrich them and impoverish us, show that *that* exigency is increasing instead of passing away. Have the monstrous exactions which were imposed upon the people in the form of protective tariff taxation, on the pretense that they were only temporary war measures, soon to be removed when the exigency of impending war had passed away, been removed, or even lightened? We all know they have not; but are supported, clung to, and advocated by the retainers of the favored few who are licensed thus to rob the masses of the people with greater pertinacity than ever.

Is the national debt which the exigencies of war fastened on the country paid? Has the interest ceased? The monthly statements of the public debt furnished by the Secretary of the Treasury show that it is not only not paid, but the principal of the interest-bearing debt has increased largely in the last four years. I have before me the statements made December 1, 1875, and December 1, 1879. The principal of the interest-bearing debt, December 1, 1875, is $1,708,251,300, the interest on which, if I have calculated it correctly, was $95,471,230 a year. On the 1st of December, 1879, the principal of the interest-bearing debt is stated by the Secretary of the Treasury at $1,786,917,650, an increase of $78,666,350 in the last four years, notwithstanding all the purchases for the sinking fund, the bonds bought therefor being destroyed as soon as purchased. The Secretary tells us, in his report to Congress on the 1st day of December last, that he has paid as interest on the public debt for the last fiscal year $105,327.949, or nearly $5,000,000 more than was required four years ago. He further informs Congress that he needs $93,877,410 to pay the interest for the current fiscal year. In the face of all these facts I would like to know from any person, whether he be judge of the Supreme Court, a member of Congress, the President of the United States, or even a New York banker, what exigency ever existed which made it constitutional for Congress to issue legal-tender notes which does not now exist to authorize Congress to continue them in circulation, with all their debt-paying capacity unimpaired.

But, Mr. President, important and immense as all these things are, they are not all nor even the greater part of the exigencies now existing which require Congress to maintain, in all their usefulness and debt-paying capacity, the legal-tender notes of the United States. Gold forms no part of our ordinary circulation. There is hardly silver coin enough of full legal-tender quality allowed to be coined at the mints, no matter how much bullion there may be in the country to furnish $1 *per capita* to each of our people; the issues of the State banks have been taxed out of existence by Federal legislation; the national-bank notes are not a legal tender in any private transaction; the debts of the States, of the municipalities, of the railroads, of the other great corporations, and of individuals, exceed the debt of the United States at least threefold. Poor's Railroad Manual for last year stated the railroad debts alone at over $2,200,000,000. I assume they are greater now, as we have built nearly four thousand miles of railway in the last twelve months. Even if the national banks were required to redeem their notes at their own counters in coin, which they are not by this resolution, it would prove to be a delusion. The banks, by their now perfect combination, could and would so assort their notes as to keep them in circulation at points far removed from home. The issues of the Kentucky banks would circulate in Minnesota and Iowa, while those of the banks of these States would be the currency of Kentucky and Tennessee. Private contracts could not be enforced. There is not a single State in the Union, except New York, in which there is a legally established United States depository where coin can be demanded on paper money.

Suppose my colleague, General WILLIAMS, contracts with me to buy my farm, my crop of wheat, hogs, or cattle, and agrees to pay me on the 1st day of March at my house, $10,000, and on payment, *on that day*, take possession of the property. He comes, according to contract, with the money in legal-tender notes. I refuse to receive them. He cannot find national-bank notes enough to draw coin from the banks in his section of country; he cannot get coin from New York in less than four days. The property has advanced in value, and I sell it next day for $12,000, and deliver it to another. When he makes the tender in coin after he gets it, I tell him that he failed to comply with his agreement on the day specified, and he has no remedy. That is the condition in which all the people of the country will be placed by the passage of a law such as this resolution proposes. It is even worse than that; the national banks will not be required to redeem their own notes at their own counters in coin if this resolution becomes the law; these notes are still to remain lawful money, just as bank-notes are now lawful money; once a debt is paid in them the plea of payment would be good on proof of payment in and acceptance of greenbacks. All the acts requiring the redemption of bank-notes provide, not for redemption in *legal-tender* notes, but in *lawful money*. Neither the Government nor any individual could demand coin from them after this resolution passes into the form of law; payment in the greenback, with its legal-tender quality destroyed, would be a compliance by the banks with all their obligations. The first section of the act of February 25, 1862, volume 12, Statutes at Large, page 345, makes the United States notes "*lawful money* and a legal tender in payment of all debts, public and private, within the United States, except duties on imports and interest on the public debt." Were these notes degraded below the rank of lawful money when, in March, 1869, notwithstanding the indorsement on their back, they were repudiated by Congress as unfit to pay the bondholders the principal of their bonds? That will not be asserted, and it is equally sure that the national banks will, if this resolution passes, continue to redeem their notes in them under their contracts or charters, because they remain "*lawful money*." Secretary Sherman, in an interview evidently prepared carefully by himself and published in the New York Herald of December 12, 1879, said, when insisting on the repeal of the legal-tender clause of the greenback notes:

The banks as heretofore under existing laws would redeem their circulating notes in United States notes.

When he says that *can* and *shall* be done, the speculations of Senators as to the construction of the resolution may as well cease; that will be the result, that is what the bankers understand; the Secretary's assurance and construction is all they ask or care for. With that construction given no man living outside of a few large cities could ever enforce compliance with any contract when payment at a given time is a condition precedent to its enforcement. The zeal of the great moneyed corporations for the degradation of the greenbacks is obvious and natural. They intend to control the currency circulation of the United States. Greenbacks with the legal-tender quality stricken out would continue to be a safe and convenient currency for them to redeem their own notes in; a run on them for coin would be impossible in that condition of things. They profess to be much afraid of inflation, and their advocates are extremely apprehensive because of the ignorance of Senators and Representatives in regard to the true interests of their constituents and the danger of reckless inflation by a foolish Congress which may overthrow and destroy all values, all industries, and all stability in business. My apprehension is from the power sought to be given to the national bankers. They can inflate the currency up to 90 per cent. of the outstanding bonds of the United States, or to $1,600,000,000, and contract it as they like when it is their interest to do so. Apprehension of the repeal of their charters while we have other currency to rely on has prevented any serious attempts in that direction so far. The $346,000,000 of legal-tender notes now nominally outstanding is the best, perhaps, with the hostility of the bankers and the Secretary of the Treasury to the issue and use of silver coin, the *only* check on national bankers and their issues; that amount cannot be curtailed or altered except after full and lengthened discussion, first in the House and next in the Senate, and after passing both Houses the bill changing the present status of the legal-tenders would have to run the gauntlet of a presidential veto, and we have all felt the power of that. The country would have full notice of the change, and would at least have ample time to prepare for it.

Strike this money down, leave us at the mercy of the national bankers, and what follows? They have an organization as compact and close as the whisky ring, the tariff ring, the railroad ring, or any other ring. They meet in convention periodically and determine, not what is best for the country, but what will most certainly put most money into their own coffers. Let them have full control of the currency of the country, and when by inflated issues of their paper promises kept in circulation in States far remote from their banking houses, most probably redeemable in United States notes not legal-tenders, they have excited the country to the highest point of wild speculation, they can by telegrams to each other, secretly, *in a single night*, when crops must be moved, when conditions exist demanding the highest possible amount of circulation, combine and contract, call in debts, refuse discounts, bankrupt the country, buy property at their own prices, and, when they get it by ruining its legitimate owners, again inflate and sell to suit themselves. Are they too patriotic and virtuous to be guilty of such acts and to take such advantages? The newspapers they pay so well may say they are, and will doubtless denounce me and other plain men who claim to be as patriotic and more dependent for future success on faithful devotion to the best interests of the people as any national banker, whether he be descended from Judas Iscariot or the unrepentent thief on the cross. I will not so vote as to place such power in the hands of any body of men who represent nobody but themselves and their stockholders, who would laugh in your face if you insisted that they ought to look beyond them and consider the rights of the people. As power and trust must be lodged somewhere, I prefer to keep and hold it in the hands of Senators and Representatives who have no other interests, can hope for no promotion except as they promote the best interests of the people they represent.

Every act of the combinations of wealth has been to impose burdens on the people in order to enrich themselves. When in time of war the legal-tenders were issued, the Government was forced to repudiate them to the extent of refusing to receive them for customs dues and interest on the public debt, so as to increase tariff taxation for the protection of favored classes up to the gold standard and make it the interest of all protected monopolists to depreciate the paper money as much below gold as possible. The bondholders alone demanded gold for their interest when all other creditors of the Government, including the soldiers and sailors, were content to take its paper promises at par. It was thus made the interest of the money-kings to raise the premium on the gold they alone could obtain as high as possible to enable them to sell their gold interest for the highest possible price; still they boast of their patriotism and the great aid they rendered the Government by lending it money on these terms. Not satisfied with that, they demanded that they alone should be allowed to control the currency of the country. For their benefit all the State banks were taxed out of existence, and they were furnished with currency as national banks up to 90 per cent. of the face value of the gold interest-bearing bonds they held, paying a tax of only 1 per cent. for it, with authority to lend it to the people at whatever rate of interest the States in which they lived allowed interest

2 BE

to be charged. Not content with even these enormous exclusive privileges, in March, 1869, they obtained from Congress a declaratory act further repudiating the legal-tender notes, each one of which had written on it by law that it should be a legal tender at its par value for all debts public and private, except interest and customs, which law declared that the principal of the bonds should be paid in coin; and in 1870 they had them exempted from all taxation, State, Federal, and municipal.

In 1873 they had silver demonetized by methods so secret and disreputable that no man has yet been found to avow that he knew when they were perpetrated. In short, every step taken has been to advance the price of gold and depreciate the value of paper money, and now these men are a unit in clamoring to destroy its legal-tender quality altogether, and denounce as repudiationists, fools, and dishonest men, all who will not obey their orders. I hope before this Congress adjourns it will require them to keep all their reserves in their own banks, or in the Treasury of the United States, and require them all to be held in gold and silver coin, and, as they seem so earnestly to desire it, require them to redeem all their own notes at their own counters in coin, on demand, and we surely ought to pass a law forbidding the issuing of any new bank charter that does not contain these provisions, providing further that there shall be no renewal or extension of existing charters to any bank until it had redeemed, in accordance with its contract, all its currency now outstanding. Many of these charters expire soon. The agreement was that they should pay back to the United States, at or before the expiration of the grants, in lawful money of the United States, as many dollars as there was circulation issued to them; not alone what might be presented for redemption. That was the only provision which was for the benefit of the people. Eight, perhaps ten, per cent. of the circulation issued has been, or in one way or another will be, destroyed in the course of the twenty years of the bank's existence under these charters. We are entitled to be paid the full amount of all the notes we issued, and have a right to the benefit of all notes destroyed. It will amount to somewhere near $30,000,000, and will go that far toward the reduction of the national debt.

The bankers and the papers they control will doubtless denounce that proposition also; but I hope Congress will not be deterred from asserting the rights of their constituents by any apprehension on that subject. Abuse is sometimes more wholesome than flattery, and rarely hurts when men are right. The banks have no just ground of complaint if we require them to pay every dollar issued to them, in accordance with their contracts, the loss by the destruction of these notes did not fall on them. They loaned out all the currency they received. If I borrowed $10,000 from one of them, and it was burned up in my house the night after I got it I had to pay the bank every dollar of it with interest. Why should the bank withhold it from the Government? *It was my loss, not theirs,* and I am more interested that the public debt should be reduced than that the bank should be paid twice, as it will be if it is not required to account for the money I paid it, and seeks to avoid payment because the Government fails to produce the destroyed notes the bank borrowed from it, which were loaned to and lost by me. Suppose five Chicago bondholders had each deposited $12,000 of their bonds, and, as national bankers, received $50,000 of national-bank currency which they had loaned out, taking good security, a day or two before the great fire in that city, and it had all been burned up. Is there any more reason why these bankers should not account for every dollar of it to the Government before they are permitted to withdraw their bonds deposited to secure the repayment of the loan of currency to them than there would be if every dollar of it was in existence? I suppose nobody will venture to say that there is. Why not pass a law at once requiring all those settlements to be made as originally agreed on, even if a new contract is entered into and a new charter granted afterward.

I am not now discussing the policy of the national-bank system, nor seeking to interfere with the privileges granted to them. I seek only to secure to the people their rights under the system, and make it work as much as possible for their interest and convenience, and I am opposing the destruction or degradation of the legal-tender notes of the United States which all citizens, State banks, and private bankers can use as currency without being dependent on national bankers for it. The absolute control of the currency of a people in the hands of a privileged few is a vast and may be a dangerous power. *I fear it.* Let me state a case to illustrate why. There may be others like it or even stronger for aught I know. I had seen in the public newspapers apparently exaggerated statements of the profits made by the First National Bank of New York; knowing that returns of the condition of the banks had to be made from time to time by them to the Comptroller of the Currency, I sent to that officer for the returns made to him by that bank for the year 1879, which he furnished me. I hold them in my hand, and they show among other things the following exhibits in the statements made on January 1, April 4, June 14, October 2, and December 12, 1879:

First. That the capital stock paid in during all that period was $500,000.

Second. That the surplus fund was $1,000,000, except on December 14, when it was $1,500,000.

Third. The undivided profits January 1, were $142,670.42; April 4, $339,095.60; June 14, $579,018.88; October 2, $804,511.26; December 12, $267,700.84—total undivided profits, $2,132,997.

Whether these undivided profits at the dates given were carried on the books as not called for from one date to another, I do not know; but if the $804,511.26 on hand October 2 represents all from January 1, 1879, it certainly shows a clear profit of $661,840.84 in nine months on a paid-in capital of $500,000—a profit sufficient to satisfy any Shylock.

Fourth. The bank had United States deposits, January 1, $24,759,948.50; April 4, $69,927,704.43; June 14, $128,109,071.04; October 2, $3,601,550.

The interest on the money belonging to the United States lying in that bank on the 4th day of June at 6 per cent. was worth to the bank over $21,000 a day. They show further in these statements among *their* liabilities to the syndicate, profit and loss—all profit, of course—independent of their other profits, *syndicate,* $2,153,959.42. All of this, recollect, was made out of a capital of only $500,000 paid in.

Mr. CONKLING. What was the profit the Senator states?

Mr. BECK. I cannot state the entire profits during the entire year with absolute certainty; but if these undivided profits are different sums, they amount to over $2,000,000. The syndicate profit and loss is $2,131,000. Whether or not they carried the statements of unpaid profits up to the next statement I am not able to say. I hope to ascertain the facts more fully hereafter. I will say, however, to the Senator from New York that before any more refunding is done, and we are now being pressed on that subject, I shall try to see how much what has been already done has cost the people of these United States in commissions and in double interest and how much it has been possible for bankers to make out of the money that has been left in their hands.

I came to the conclusion, looking over these statements, that the best banking capital a man can have is the good-will and patronage of the Secretary of the Treasury. Suppose the Senator from New York were the best banker and I were to go to him and say, "I want to go into partnership with you;" and the Senator should say to me. "What capital have you got?" "None." "What business experience have you got?" "None." "What do you propose to do?" "I propose to bring you the good-will and the deposits of the Secretary." I think the Senator would take me into partnership and he would make more money by doing it than he ever made in his life, and we could contribute largely to any campaign fund desired by the Secretary.

I do not say that any of these things have been done; but I say a system under which they are possible is a vicious system and dangerous to liberty, and one that I shall try to suppress if I can. In any other loans that are made I shall endeavor to make it impossible for the Treasury of the United States to be used to aid one set of bankers against another set of bankers, or to allow the money of the people to be used in the business of anybody, any more than I would allow them to aid one manufacturer against another or one shipbuilder against another, or any other class of men anywhere, with the money belonging to this people.

Mr. MORRILL. Will the Senator from Kentucky allow me to interrupt him for the purpose of making some correction of his statement?

Mr. BECK. If I have made any wrong statement, of course.

Mr. MORRILL. The Senator represents the First National Bank to be a bank of a capital in the first place of only $500,000.

Mr. BECK. I have their own statement in my hand which says so.

Mr. MORRILL. The Senator will find that the capital of the bank originally was $500,000; that they have an accession to it of undivided surplus of $1,277,000 in addition; that they paid in taxes last year $237,479.63; and that another fact is, that the Secretary of the Treasury never deposited a single dollar in the bank. All that was deposited there was deposited by subscribers to the loan.

Mr. BECK. I did not say——

Mr. MORRILL. And they have——

Mr. BECK. Mr. President, I decline to be further interrupted.

The PRESIDING OFFICER, (Mr. EATON in the chair.) The Senator from Kentucky declines to be interrupted.

Mr. MORRILL. It is a matter that ought to be understood.

Mr. BECK. I have made no charge against the Secretary. I say these profits were made out of this capital of $500,000; that they had a surplus of $1,000,000 at the beginning of the year, and $1,500,000 at the end of it, besides all these profits, and a syndicate profit of over $2,000,000.

Mr. MORRILL. But they negotiated $268,000,000, and did not make more than $\frac{8}{10}$ of 1 per cent. on what business they did in that respect.

Mr. BECK. Any system that enables one set of men to do that thing is a vicious system, and they are not the kind of men into whose hands we ought to place all the money and the currency of the United States, with power to control it as they please.

I will not aid in strengthening or in building up a system under which such favoritism, such subsidies, such discriminations, call them what you will, is not only possible, but is certain to arise and grow in magnitude as power is increased.

I think the passage of the resolution under consideration strongly tends to the perpetuation and extension of this condition of things, and shall therefore vote against it.

I will try in the future to give the people a chance to obtain bonds directly from the Government authorities by paying for them at any depository, instead of enriching a few men at the public expense. I will not discuss that now, however.

But, Mr. President, I would oppose the passage of the resolution at this time, independent of all these difficulties and dangers, on the ground that we have not yet regained permanent prosperity, and are not likely to do so until many of our laws are changed.

So long as our present barbarous navigation laws are maintained and our people are the only people upon earth who are not permitted to buy ships where they can buy them cheapest—indeed, are not permitted to buy them anywhere abroad—we must continue to be a poor, dependent, subsidiary nation on the great highways of commerce and pay to foreign nations, as we do now, over $100,000,000 a year to do our carrying trade. We might as well abandon all hope of greatness while these laws exist. The miserable falsehood that we are protecting home industry against pauper labor, which sounds so well, is best answered by the fact that we are building no foreign ocean-going steamers, and that not a single ship in any of the great lines from the great port of New York which cross the Atlantic is an American ship or carries the American flag. The few we have anywhere were built by taxation in the shape of subsidies, while the protected monopoly of the coastwise trade excludes all competition there, so that the home ship-owners can charge what they please. In short, we have surrendered our great foreign trade to foreign monopoly to secure the coastwise trade to home monopoly, the mass of this people, producers and consumers alike, being taxed to bear the burdens of both, while American labor is destroyed by (so-called) protection in our foreign trade.

The Secretary of the Treasury in his last report to Congress, page 28, stated that our small tonnage engaged in the foreign trade decreased last year 137,514 tons below what it was the year before. Only 23 per cent. of our combined imports and exports are carried in American ships; over 75 per cent. in foreign. Twenty years ago over 75 per cent. was carried in American ships. The Secretary adds:

It is neither to the advantage nor the honor of the country that so immense a proportion of its foreign carrying trade has passed to other nations. * * * It is a grave question of public policy whether the period has not arrived when the unlimited right of purchase, as under the English statutes, should be extended to vessels as well as to other commodities.

I am glad the Secretary has called the attention of Congress to this subject, as I believe its time could be spent much more profitably in the passage of the bill I have before the Senate, to allow us to have free ships, than in passing resolutions to cripple our means of paying for them. Our high protective tariff is a confession that we do not intend to try to manufacture goods to sell outside of the limits of the United States. Our manufacturers are content with the tribute Congress authorizes them to levy from our own people. We boast of our wonderful ingenuity, and are justly proud of our magnificent machinery; we protect by patent monopolies all inventions. What does it all amount to ? Only this: each improved machine is the slave of its owner, requiring no clothing and cheap food, if any; it performs the work of many human beings and drives them out of employment. Yet the price to consumers is kept up by combination among machine-owners and by tariff taxation on all outside who dare to compete. All the people in the world wear clothes which cost them 50 per cent. less than the people of the United States and sleep under blankets 50 per cent. cheaper than ours. None of these facts appear in the false reports we are periodically flooded with, which tell us how much cheaper men can buy corn, flour, bacon, petroleum, butter, eggs, and food generally here than elsewhere, and call eatables the cost of living, when they are less than one-fourth of it. Let us examine this *great boom of prosperity* which the bankers, bondholders, and their allies attribute to resumption, and on the strength of which they seek to strike down, as though all danger was past, the legal-tender money of the country. Has our commerce or carrying trade increased? *No.* Are we sending more of our manufactures to other countries? *No;* but we were blessed with bounteous harvests; abundance prevailed in all our land. Other nations were cursed with blighted crops, and scarcity existed everywhere else. Our producers realized good prices; our transportation routes of all sorts were taxed to their utmost capacity; others were laid out and put in operation. The money received was freely invested and expended; confidence was restored as men's pockets were filled. In short, we were blessed in the proportion that other people in other countries were cursed.

The balance of trade was in our favor, of course it was. Protective tariffs prevented men who sold wheat, flour, and beef abroad from buying what they needed elsewhere; they were compelled to pay 50 per cent. more at home; but that brought the money here, inflated the currency, stimulated trade, and, while it was robbery of the producer, he had done so well he did not grumble. Reverse these providential conditions next year, let abundant crops prevail over Europe and scarcity in agricultural products prevail here, and all the conditions of our present prosperity would disappear more rapidly than they sprang up, as nine-tenths of our exports have been simply food in one form or other, or raw materials put in shape for cheap transportation. Have we as legislators any right to assume that the exceptional conditions of last year will continue? Surely not. Therefore it seems to me to be sheer folly to interfere with our currency on the assumption that it will; and it is absolutely certain that whenever we cannot send abroad unprotected and unprotectable agricultural products the balance of trade, even under our artificial high protective tariff, is gone. We may keep up a semblance of it by applying the same rule to all other things that we now do to ships—absolutely prohibit our people from purchasing anything abroad; then, if we can sell *anything* to foreign nations, all the so-called balance of trade will be in our favor, and our politicians may continue to deceive ignorant people. The protective system of robbery is better than highway robbery in this, the victims are not conscious of the wrong, and they can be made to enjoy the swindle by being induced to believe that they are patriotic in their sacrifices.

I cannot refrain from reading in this connection, as it applies with equal force to the tariff robbery as it does to the ship-building folly, an extract from a letter written by one of the wisest, perhaps *the wisest*, living statesman in America, Hon. Horatio Seymour, to Hon. Erastus Brooks, a short time ago. He said:

There is no reason entitled to respect to be given for our navigation laws so far as they forbid our merchants to buy ships elsewhere for the purposes of foreign trade. The governments of Europe, more wise, do what they can to build up their commerce, and their flags are seen in our harbors waving over vessels bought by their merchants where they can get them upon the best terms. Every such flag seems to reproach the folly of laws which practically forbid American citizens to carry American produce across the ocean, or to share in the great profits of the world's commerce. There is an alarm about communistic principles. What are they? Some wild theorists claim that it is the duty of government to give labor to workmen, and to take care that property shall be so held in common that what one earns may be given to another. We frown upon these men and denounce their purposes. But what do they claim more than a few builders of steamships get under our navigation laws? These demand that all such vessels for foreign trade must be made by them; that the buyer, besides paying for what they are worth, must divide some of his property with the builders by giving them more than they are worth in the markets of the world. It will be found in the end that communism, which lurks in laws which force men to buy of certain classes, and to pay more for what they want than they can be bought for elsewhere, and which also divide men's estates under cover of taxation, which indirectly go to favored individuals, is more hurtful and dangerous than the communism which says what it means, and which destroys itself by an open declaration of its purposes.

That is a brave, manly statement of a great truth, and I may as well here as anywhere illustrate why I so emphatically indorse it. All the professions of the opponents of free ships, of the subsidy-seekers, of the protective tariff monopolists, are based on the assumption that they seek to protect American labor against foreign pauper competition. Their zeal for the maintenance of a high rate of wages and constant employment to workingmen constitute the staple of their appeals to Congress for the perpetuation of the systems they advocate; yet in the face of all these professions the great ship-yards which used to resound with the sound of the adze and the hammer in constructing our ships are all closed and the thousands of skilled mechanics once employed there are tramps or driven into other employments. I have seen the oldest and best of the salt-works of America on the Kanawha, in West Virginia, closed and the laborers and their families reduced to starvation under a contract with other protected companies, which paid the owners many thousands of dollars annually as *dead rent*, to prevent competition with the other companies and enable them by combination, protected by a tariff of 100 per cent., to tax every human being in the land for the salt they were compelled to use, and they clamored all the time for the protection of American labor.

I hold in my hand a letter from an intelligent gentleman in Saint Louis, Missouri, written a few days ago in answer to an inquiry as to the arrangement by which the "Vulcan Iron Works" in that city were closed. At least eight hundred men used to be employed there, many of them mechanics and skilled laborers; at the usual average of five to a family they represented four thousand human beings. He says:

I learned to-day that each of the Bessemer companies pays $1 a ton into the pool for all steel manufactured by them. The Vulcan received $70,000 last year as a *bonus* for stopping their furnaces, besides the $70,000, their proportion in the pool; so their income last year was $140,000 from Bessemer companies alone. This was given in a general conversation with one of their directors.

That is a specimen of the protection given by Congress and its pets to American labor; it is the protection given to the lamb by the wolf; $140,000 a year paid to a few rich men as the price of starving four thousand people. A system under which such things are possible must be vicious. Mr. J. S. Moore, who is known to many Senators as one of the most intelligent writers on the subject of taxation, in a letter addressed to the Committee of Ways and Means of the House of Representatives, January 3, 1880, explains how these bounties can be paid to avoid competition or a reduction of combination prices. He says:

> I shall again direct your attention to-day to the great glaring tariff oppression practiced in levying $28 duty on a ton of steel rails. Behold in two lines again the great outrage on a free people:
>
> Price of steel rails in the United States........................ $70 to $73 per ton.
> Price of English steel rails in Liverpool, £8.................... 40   per ton.
>
> Difference 30   per ton.
>
> Thus you see the duty of $28 a ton gives our American monopolists the full pound of flesh.
>
> * * * * * * *
>
> Yet you keep bound over to the avarice and monopoly of an organized steel-rail association more than eighty thousand miles of railway, and forty-five millions of people, who eventually must pay for this increased price on steel rails.
>
> The producers of the soil whose markets are at a distance naturally demand cheap rates of freight from railways. Above all, they desire new roads that can be cheaply built. But if, by a direct piece of class legislation, eleven corporations are given a monopoly of $28 tariff royalty on a ton of steel rails, the farmers as well as the great consumers are simply oppressed by such a law.
>
> * * * * * * *
>
> Is it not self-evident that in this short-lived passage of the prosperity "boom" the people are again creating works on an inflated basis? And is it true or is it false that the shameful duty of $28 a ton on steel rails is directly inflating every mile of steel rails (calculated at one hundred tons to the mile) with $2,800 on account of the tariff alone? Let it be remembered also that the steel-rail production of the United States is second only to that of Great Britain, and it is even boasted that in this respect it will surpass that country this very year of 1880. Surely, the great steel-rail works of the United States will not be foolish enough to plead the baby act, or the usual plea of an industrial infancy.
>
> In conclusion, I will only say that keeping the present duty on steel rails is simply equivalent to legislating some $28,000,000 to $30,000,000 per annum into the pockets of eleven steel-rail corporations, pressed out from the consumers of the great, the free, the prosperous, and the tariff-ridden people of the United States.

I am not making war specially on the iron interest. I would reduce the protection to the revenue point, and that would be ample. All the other monopolies of silk, wool, &c., are just as bad. I use these illustrations now only to show that we can and do only cheat ourselves and each other by our vicious legislation. We cannot extort from any other people in the world any higher prices for our manufactures than any other nation is willing to sell like articles for; therefore we have little or no export trade in manufactures and can have none, no commerce, no ships, nothing except what starving people abroad, in a year of bad harvests, were obliged at any sacrifice to buy from us; and as we could not trade with them, no matter how badly we wanted, for example, their railroad iron, we had to demand money, come home, and pay $30 per ton more for the same article; and that is the lauded balance of trade in our favor, from which no revenue to support the Government is derived; upon the strength of which we are at once to declare permanent prosperity, throw our legal-tenders to the winds, surrender all our currency to the national bankers, or be denounced as repudiators if we hesitate.

I have examined the detailed report of the Bureau of Statistics in the Treasury Department for the first nine months of the year 1879, and compared our exports and imports during that period with those of the corresponding months of the year 1878, and I fail to find anything in them to give assurance of continued commercial prosperity.

Our exports from January 1 to October 1, 1878, were.. $528,696,334
And for the same period in 1879 509,508,519

A falling off of 19,187,815

Our imports for that period in 1879 were............... $355,736,481
And for the same period in 1878 324,611,718

  Excess in 1879 over 1878......................... 31,124,763

So that we have really been exporting less and importing more last year than the year preceding by $50,000,000. I said we were only sustained by the accidental demand for bread in other countries. A few plain facts prove it:

From January 1 to October 1, 1879, we exported of
 wheat and flour...................................... $140,406,861
In 1878, same period 110,303,439

  Excess in 1879 over 1878......................... 30,103,422

In September, 1879, we exported of wheat and flour... 64,726,058
In September, 1878..... 57,413,273

  Excess in September, 1879......................... 7,316,785

From these facts, and many others I might state, it is painfully apparent that our trade and commerce is not increasing. We export no manufactures of woolens, only a few of the commonest cotton goods, nothing worthy of the name of manufactures, while our imports of staple goods, even under the high protective tariff, are increasing, mainly by reason of the enormous price asked now, under the so-called boom, by home producers. As specimens: the imports of woolen dress goods have increased for nine months in 1879 over 1878, $2,000,000; silk dress goods, over $3,500,000; manufactures of cotton, over $3,000,000, and so with other staples. In short, we are falling off in all things except what people must have to eat, and our imports are increasing by reason of the enormous profits asked for all manufactured articles at home. Even the so-called balance of trade is a mere temporary chance to steal from the products of the farmers a large portion of their profits by forcing them, while they must sell in open competition abroad, unprotected, to buy from protected monopolies here. Refined sugar seems to be the principal article the export of which is increasing; it shows over $3,500,000 gain in 1879 over 1878; that is another trick; the melado, or sugar from which it is made, is imported as the lowest grade at the minimum duty, and the highest duty collected on the highest grade is refunded when it is refined and exported; so that our apparent prosperity in that increase of business is only an increase in a costly and successful fraud.

It is a humiliating fact that every pretended advancement of the interests of the people by Congress in the last twenty years has been in the interest of combinations of wealth and against the interest of the toiling masses. *Who would work if he could be a banker, favored with Government deposits as the First National Bank of New York has been?* What manufacturer cares to compete for the commerce of the world when Congress compels our own people to pay him and his comrades whatever they see fit to ask for their goods? What stability can there be in business when profits are secured by legislation instead of competition—profits so great that everybody who can rushes into the business, gluts the home market, and refuse or are unable to take such prices as the balance of the world pays? What good did our great land grants to railroads do the people when we erected by law barriers against receiving the products of the countries we professed such anxiety to reach? Taxes for subsidies, taxes for protection, taxes for everything, seems to be the height to which statesmanship aspires. Perhaps I have said enough to show why I do not believe in the argument in favor of the passage of the resolution, which is based on the claim of the assured permanent prosperity of the country. If I could see American ships on the high seas earning and keeping at home the $100,000,000 we are now annually paying to foreign nations; if I could see our manufactures of wool, cotton, and iron exported to supply the wants of South America, China, and Japan, bringing back to us the products of these countries at the same prices other nations obtain them, to furnish material for our workshops, I would have great confidence in an assured prosperity. So long as all these things are made impossible by vicious legislation, I am not prepared to interfere with the present usefulness of the notes of the United States. If the time comes, as it may in the future under better laws, that an honest, not a forced balance of trade in our favor, earned by our superior ingenuity and skill, when we are drawing coin and obtaining credit from other nations in a reasonably assured continuance of exchange of commodities—for all trade in the end is barter—and when the people are allowed to coin their silver as freely as they now can their gold, I may consent to withdraw all our promises to pay; but I must see all these things ahead much more clearly than I do now, before I turn the money of this people over absolutely to the tender mercy of the national-bankers. The truth is, we are a combination and a corporation ridden people. I do not propose, in this condition of things, to surrender all our currency to the great banking corporations; its proposed degradation means its speedy destruction; its refusal at the custom-house, by the banks, by all the corporations and combinations of wealth opposed to it. It would be at a discount at once in the hands of the people just as the trade-dollar, though more valuable intrinsically than the standard dollar, is; because it has no legal-tender quality, and is that far repudiated by Congress. Of course so-called resumption will be maintained, if the Secretary has to sell $500,000,000 of 5 per cent. bonds to do it, as he claims the right to do under the resumption act. Nothing but the exhaustion of the credit of the country can stop that. It was accomplished by the bankruptcy of thousands and the impoverishment of millions of the people. It could have been effected years before without any such results if the silver coinage had not been clandestinely stricken down and the legal-tender notes had been accepted at the custom-house. It became possible at last only by the even restricted restoration of silver to the coinage, and the reception in violation of law of legal-tenders for customs dues. The moment the greenback is destroyed, as now proposed, war will be re-opened with redoubled force against silver, and we will be again reduced to the gold standard and to the tender mercy of the bankers and bondholders. The fact that all public and private debts can be paid in silver coin—and all interest on bonds is by law payable in it when it is taken for customs taxes—makes it impossible for bondholders to demand gold. They know it; and their zeal in behalf of this resolution grows out of the fact that they regard it as a great stride in the direction of the firm establishment of the single gold standard. It is simply a continuation of a struggle that always has existed, and never will cease while liberty lasts—the efforts of wealth and privileges to bring the toiling masses to their feet, and the resistance of the people against the encroachments of power. The contest is unequal. It is trained and well-paid regulars against untrained and unorganized militia.

I have never knowingly struck a blow in my political career that was not aimed against the greedy combinations of wealth seeking advantages. If we can prolong the contest a little while longer the representation from the great agricultural regions will be felt as it has never been before on these great questions, and the tone of men from the protected and favored regions will be less arrogant than now.

When at the first session of this Congress we had the courage, without consulting or waiting for reports from committees, to put quinine on a free list, a howl of indignation went up from the protected monopolists. I was honored with printed circulars and anonymous letters telling me what fools and knaves we all were, and especially what an idiot I was for the part I had taken in it. What has happened? Mr. Moore, in the letter I read from previously, says:

The thanks and acknowledgment for this boon belong to the House of Representatives and Senate direct, without the intervention of committees. As members of Congress, therefore, allow me to congratulate you on the result, which I will give you in two lines:

	Per oz.
Price of quinine January 2, 1879, duty 20 per cent	$3 70
Price of quinine January 2, 1880, free of duty	2 60
Reduction	1 10

I need not dwell on the sound policy of having freed quinine from a duty. The fever-smitten millions and the hospitals will and do surely feel the full force of the foregoing two lines. Nor have Messrs. Powers & Weightman and Rosengarten & Sons ceased to manufacture quinine. On the contrary, they are nobly holding their own in full competition with the so-called pauper quinine of Europe.

Senators must not forget that a majority of the common laborers of this country work for less than $12 a month. It cost them each more than two days' hard labor to earn the $1.10 which Congress had for so many years forced them to pay to two or three of the Philadelphia pet monopolists before they were allowed to buy an ounce of quinine to save their own lives or those of their stricken wives and children. Do not forget that by that one little act we saved more than four days' hard work to every cook and house-girl—because they rarely get over $6 a month—on each ounce of quinine she is obliged to buy; and the comfort of that reflection will be a full recompense for all the abuse of the metropolitan press, or of the advocates of all such monopolies; and there are hundreds of them still left.

Let Senators ask themselves how have the colossal fortunes which have sprung up like mushrooms in this country been amassed. Did these men trade with the people of other nations, and by superior skill, energy, or intelligence bring home the money made out of them? No; they made them *out of congressional legislation*, which, under the name and guise of protection in one form or other, protected them not against foreigners, but against the right of the people of the United States to buy anything without paying heavy tribute to the favored combination. Examine into the business of any of them, from the First National Bank of New York to the Bessemer steel monopolies. All their vast profits grow out of class legislation. All they make is wrung from the toiling millions at home. There are fourteen hundred million of people outside of the United States; only fifty million inside. Why is it impossible for the fifty million of Americans to trade with the fourteen hundred million? Simply and only because the favored few in our own midst have so arranged congressional legislation as to give them the control of all our business and the right to make us pay what they please for everything we must have. Now, when, by the blessing of Providence, and in spite of legislation, the farmers of the country have drawn large sums of money in open market from foreign nations in return for food, they are at once told they have too much money; that it must be destroyed; that they will overspeculate and break themselves; that the bankers alone can be trusted to regulate how much money they shall be allowed to have, and what shall be its character. I shall continue to resist all such assumptions, of which I think this resolution will prove to be one of the most pronounced.

Printed by Libri Plureos GmbH in Hamburg,
Germany